L. A. HILL

ELEMENTARY COMPREHENSION PIECES

LONDON
OXFORD UNIVERSITY PRESS

Oxford University Press, Ely House, London W.1

GLASGOW NEW YORK TORONTO MELBOURNE WELLINGTON
CAPE TOWN SALISBURY IBADAN NAIROBI DAR ES SALAAM LUSAKA
ADDIS ABABA BOMBAY CALCUTTA MADRAS KARACHI LAHORE DACCA
KUALA LUMPUR SINGAPORE HONG KONG TOKYO

ISBN 0 19 432511 3

© Oxford University Press, 1963

First published 1963
Eighth impression 1971

Reprinted by offset in Great Britain by
Alden & Mowbray Ltd
at the Alden Press, Oxford

CONTENTS

	page			page
INTRODUCTION	3	16.	The Football Match	34
1. Swimming	4	17.	The Thief	36
2. The Picnic	6	18.	Our Playground	38
3. Jim's Stomach-ache	8	19.	Hobbies	40
4. My Bees	10	20.	In the Kitchen	42
5. Our Zoo	12	21.	A Party	44
6. Marbles	14	22.	At the Barber's	46
7. Aeroplanes	16	23.	At the Dentist's	48
8. The Cinema	18	24.	An Accident	50
9. In a Boat	20	25.	In Hospital	52
10. My Uncle's Farm	22	26.	In the Office	54
11. Cows	24	27.	Cycling	56
12. Fishing	26	28.	Climbing Mountains	58
13. Photographs	28		A Thousand Word Vocabulary	60
14. The Battle	30			
15. Snow!	32			

INTRODUCTION

This book contains twenty-eight pieces, each about 200 words in length and written within the limits of the 1,000 word vocabulary which appears in the Appendix. Grammatical structures are limited to a corresponding level: for instance, no conditionals, passives, relative clauses, reported speech or modal auxiliaries are used; and tenses are limited to the present simple, the present continuous, the present perfect, the simple future with *will*, the *going to* future, the past simple and the past continuous. The questions after each piece test comprehension *only*; they do not test the composition skill at all.

1 SWIMMING

When I was a boy, I liked swimming very much. One year my two brothers and I spent the summer holidays with my uncle and aunt in their house by the sea. It was only twenty yards from the water. Every day we put on our swimming-shorts before breakfast, ran down to the sea across the sand and jumped in. From then until late at night, we were in the sea or on the beach most of the time. When our aunt rang a bell, we went back to the house for food, but we ate it in our swimming-shorts and were soon back in the sea again.

The water was warm, the sun shone every day, and on most days there were no waves. In the middle of the day a wind always began to blow, but it was not strong and did not make the sea rough.

Three times during our holidays we had strong winds. They blew the sand against our legs when we ran down to the sea, and made big waves with white tops. We were all very good swimmers. We dived through the waves or rode towards the beach on top of them until we were tired and hungry.

QUESTIONS

1 Put one word from this story in each empty place in these sentences:
 a The boys wore .... in the sea.
 b The strong winds made .... on the sea.
 c The beach between the sea and the house had .... on it.
 d On most days the sea was not ....
 e The boys did not spend much time in the .... during the day.

2 Find words in the story which mean the opposite of:
 (a) smooth (b) full (c) weak (d) little (e) cold.

3 Choose the right sentence from (a), the right sentence from (b), etc.
 a The boys' home was near the sea.
   Their uncle's home was near the sea.
   Their uncle's home was a long way from the water.
 b The boys had breakfast on the sand.
   The boys did not have breakfast.
   The boys had breakfast in the house.
 c The boys put on their swimming-shorts before each meal.
   The boys put other clothes on before every meal.
   The boys did not do anything to their clothes before meals.
 d There was a wind every day.
   There was a wind on three days.
   There was a wind on most days.
 e The waves rode on top of the boys towards the beach.
   The waves carried the boys towards the beach.
   The boys rode on top of their brothers towards the beach.

2 THE PICNIC

It was Sunday and the weather was fine, so Mrs Smith said, "Let's go for a picnic." "Oh, yes!" said Mary and John, her two children. Mr Smith said, "Yes, let us go to the woods and have our picnic there." "Good," said Mrs Smith, "Help me to get the things ready." "All right," said the children. John brought the basket for the food and the bottles for the water; and Mary brought a blanket, while Mother made the sandwiches, and Father put water and oil into the car.

Soon everything was ready and they left the house. They drove along small roads until they came to the woods. Mary put the blanket on the ground, John took the food out of the car, Father made a fire, and Mother made tea.

"Isn't it beautiful here?" said Mother. "It's very quiet and green." John had a kite, and soon he was running across the grass with it. "Be careful!" shouted Mother, but it was too late! John fell over the basket of food, and everything fell out. "Look!" cried Mary. "There are ants in the food!" Yes, there were! There were hundreds of them. The blanket was on an ants' nest!

QUESTIONS

1 Put one word from this story in each empty place in these sentences:
a Mrs Smith had two ....
b The Smiths had a picnic in the ....
c The Smiths' water for making tea was in ....
d John fell over the basket because he was playing with his......... .
e The ants came from their ....

2 Find words in the story which mean the opposite of:
(*a*) careless (*b*) ugly (*c*) early (*d*) cloudy (*e*) noisy

3 Choose the right sentence from (*a*), the right sentence from (*b*), etc.
a When the Smiths went for their picnic, it was raining.
When the Smiths went for their picnic, the sun was shining.
When the Smiths went for their picnic, it was a cloudy day.
b Both children helped their mother to get the things ready.
Only John helped his mother.
Only Mary helped her mother.
c They had their picnic near the water.
They had their picnic in the woods.
They had their picnic along small roads.
d John fell out of the basket.
John's kite fell out of the basket.
The food fell out of the basket.
e Mary put the blanket on an ants' nest.
John put the blanket on an ants' nest.
The ants' nest was on the blanket.

3 JIM'S STOMACH-ACHE

Jim went to the doctor this morning. He likes apples very much and yesterday he ate too many green ones, so this morning he had a stomach-ache. When he came to breakfast he was crying. "What's the matter, Jim?" his mother said. "Why are you crying?" "My stomach hurts, Mother," he answered. "You ate too many apples yesterday," she said, "and they were green. Go to Dr Jones and he will give you some medicine. You know his house." "Yes, Mother. I'll go in the bus. And I don't want any breakfast now."

Jim got to Dr Jones's house at 9.30, but there were four other people in the doctor's waiting-room, so Jim didn't see the doctor until about 10 o'clock. "What's the matter with you, young man?" said Dr Jones. "I have a stomach-ache," said Jim. "Have you eaten any green apples?" asked the doctor. "Yes, I ate a lot yesterday," Jim said, and smiled. The doctor smiled too. He wrote on a piece of paper and said, "Take this to a chemist, and he will give you some medicine." Jim thanked the doctor, went to a chemist and bought the medicine. His stomach-ache was soon better.

QUESTIONS

1 Put one word from this story in each empty place in these sentences:
a Jim ate a lot of green ....
b He was crying because he had a ....
c He went to the doctor's house in a ....
d The doctor gave Jim a piece of ....
e The .... made Jim's stomach-ache better.

2 Find words in the story which mean about the same as:
(a) pain (b) trouble (c) loves (d) quickly (e) a lot of.

3 Choose the right sentence from (a), the right sentence from (b), etc.
a Jim went to the doctor because he did not want any breakfast.
Jim went to the doctor because he didn't want any medicine.
Jim went to the doctor because he had a pain.
b Jim saw the doctor before four other people.
Jim saw the doctor with four other people.
Jim saw the doctor after four other people.
c The doctor gave Jim some medicine for his stomach-ache.
The doctor gave Jim a piece of paper.
The doctor gave Jim some apples.
d The doctor wrote the name of a medicine on a piece of paper.
The doctor wrote the name of a chemist on the piece of paper.
The doctor wrote only his name on the piece of paper.
e Jim bought the medicine from a chemist.
Jim brought the medicine to a chemist.
Jim took the doctor to a chemist.

4 MY BEES

I live in the country, and there is a large garden round my house. I have a lot of bees in this garden, and they make honey for me. It is very good honey, because there are a lot of flowers in my garden, and the bees make their honey from these flowers. Sometimes a bee stings me, but I don't mind. When I collect the honey, I wear a net over my face and cover my hands. Then the bees do not sting me.

When I have collected a lot of honey, I put it in pots and take most of it to the town. I put a small table at the side of the road and put my pots of honey on it. Then I shout, "Honey! Beautiful honey! Who wants my sweet honey?" My honey is not expensive, and soon I have sold all the pots.

Of course, I keep some of my bees' honey at home, and my family and I eat it. We never buy any honey or jam in the shops, because my wife makes all our jam from the fruit in our garden. It tastes much better than the jam from shops, we think.

QUESTIONS

1 Put one word from this story in each empty place in these sentences:
a When bees .... people, it hurts.
b If you put a .... over you, bees do not sting you.
c I sell my honey in .... , not in bottles.
d I sell my honey in the .... , not in the country.
e Honey has a very .... taste.

2 Find words in the story which mean the opposite of:
(a) worse (b) small (c) cheap (d) sour (e) bought.

3 Choose the right sentence from (a), the right sentence from (b), etc.
a I keep bees in the country.
  I keep bees in a town.
  I keep bees in the country and in the town.
b When I wear a net, the bees do not sting me.
  The bees never sting me.
  The bees never sting my hands.
c I sell my honey in a shop.
  I sell my honey in the street.
  I sell my honey at home.
d I sell all my honey.
  I sell a little of my honey.
  I sell most of my honey.
e My family and I like jam from the shops best.
  My family and I like our jam best.
  My family and I do not eat jam. We eat honey instead.

5 OUR ZOO

Jane's class is going to visit the zoo tomorrow. Our town has a big zoo with lots of animals in it. There are some beautiful tigers and two old lions. Lions and tigers are fierce animals, so when they are in zoos, they live in strong cages. They eat a lot of meat every day.

There are also two big elephants and a baby one. Jane wants to ride on one of the elephants. The elephants are tame and kind. They eat a lot of grass every day. They like children because they sometimes give them bread and bananas. Elephants like bananas very much.

In our zoo there are also brown bears, black bears and white bears. They stand on their back legs, hold up their arms and ask for food. They like cake very much.

There is also a Children's Corner in our zoo. There children ride horses and donkeys and watch the monkeys. The monkeys are very funny. They climb up ropes and jump down again and play with each other like small children. They love nuts and bananas and bread. Jane is going to take a basket to the zoo with stale bread, cake, nuts and a bunch of bananas.

QUESTIONS

1 Put one word from this story in each empty place in these sentences:
a Jane is going to visit the zoo with her ………. .
b One of the elephants is a ………. .
c The bears love ………. .
d Children can ride donkeys in the ………. ………. .
e Jane is going to take some food to the zoo for the ………. .

2 Find words in the story which mean the opposite of:
(a) hate (b) fresh (c) wild (d) big (e) front.

3 Choose the right sentence from (a), the right sentence from (b), etc.
a Jane is going to visit the zoo alone.
  Jane is going to visit the zoo with other pupils.
  Jane is not going to visit the zoo tomorrow.
b Lions live in strong cages because they are fierce.
  Lions live in strong cages because they are animals.
  Lions live in strong cages because they eat a lot of meat.
c Bears love cake.
  Bears like bananas very much.
  Bears don't like cake very much.
d Children watch the monkeys.
  Horses watch the monkeys.
  Donkeys watch the monkeys.
e Jane is going to get bread, cake, nuts and bananas in the zoo.
  Jane is going to take bread, cake, nuts and bananas to the zoo.
  Jane is going to take bread, cake, nuts and bananas from the zoo.

6 MARBLES

The boys in our town often play marbles, and sometimes the girls play too. My brother George plays marbles very well. He has won 112 marbles in two months. He plays better than any of the other boys in our street. He shoots the marbles very straight and hits the other boys' marbles almost every time, although he is only ten years old.

When the boys in our town play marbles, they first draw a circle on the ground with a stick, and then one boy puts one of his marbles in it. Then the other boy shoots at it with one of *his* marbles and tries to knock it out of the circle. It is not easy, because the marbles are quite small, and the ground is never quite flat. When I play marbles with George, my marbles usually roll to one side or the other, and he wins.

George has marbles of all colours. Some are white like milk, some are green, some blue, some red and some yellow; and some have no colour, like glass in a window. George is teaching our small brother Dick to play marbles. Dick will learn to play well, I think; and then George will give him all his marbles and stop playing.

QUESTIONS

1 Put one word from this story in each empty place in these sentences:
a The girls sometimes play .... in our town.
b George is my ....
c When the boys play marbles, they always put one marble in a ....
d George .... the other boy's marble out of the circle almost every time.
e I do not play marbles ....

2 Find words in this story which mean the opposite of:
(a) seldom (b) loses (c) begin (d) worse (e) always.

3 Choose the right sentence from (a), the right sentence from (b), etc.
a George usually loses when he plays marbles.
George usually wins when he plays marbles.
George has stopped playing marbles.
b When I play marbles with George, I usually knock his marbles out of the circle.
When I play marbles with George, I seldom knock his marbles out of the circle.
When I play marbles with George, I never knock his marbles out of the circle.
c I play marbles better than George does.
George plays marbles better than I do.
I play marbles as well as George does.
d George's marbles have no colour.
All George's marbles have a colour.
Some of George's marbles are like glass in a window.
e George will stop playing marbles.
Dick will stop playing marbles.
I will stop playing marbles.

7 AEROPLANES

Singapore
Wednesday, 28th September

Have you ever been in an aeroplane? *I* have. Last Monday I flew to Singapore. Twelve days ago I went to the office in Kuala Lumpur and bought my ticket. Then, very early on Monday morning, I went to the office again with my luggage and got into the bus with the other passengers.

The bus took us to the airport. There people took our luggage and put it in the aeroplane, and then, after about twenty minutes, we got in too. I was a little afraid at first, because it was my first ride in an aeroplane, but a kind lady (she was the air-hostess) brought us some sweets and spoke to me, and soon I was quite happy again.

Then the captain of the aeroplane came and spoke to me too. That made me afraid again. "Is nobody driving the aeroplane?" I asked. The captain laughed kindly and said, "Another officer is there. Don't be afraid."

We flew over some clouds. They were very white, like cotton-wool, and beautiful. Then we began to come down because we were near Singapore. We went through the clouds and flew over Singapore. It was very interesting. When we got out of the aeroplane, I said, "I like flying!"

QUESTIONS

1 Put one word from this story in each empty place in these sentences:
a I went from the office to the airport in a ....
b There were other .... in the bus.
c The air-hostess gave the passengers ....
d When the captain came and spoke to me, it made me ....
e The aeroplane flew through some ....

2 Find words in this story which mean about the same as:
(*a*) also (*b*) frightened (*c*) above (*d*) pretty (*e*) bags.

3 Choose the right sentence from (*a*), the right sentence from (*b*), etc.
a I bought my ticket on Monday morning.
  I bought my ticket twelve days ago.
  The office bought my ticket.
b We put our luggage in the aeroplane.
  Others put our luggage in the aeroplane.
  The other passengers put my luggage in the aeroplane.
c I have often been in an aeroplane.
  I have never been in an aeroplane.
  I have been in an aeroplane once.
d The air-hostess made me feel happy.
  The air-hostess frightened me.
  I did not see the air-hostess.
e The aeroplane went through the clouds because they were beautiful.
  The aeroplane went through the clouds because it was near Singapore.
  The aeroplane went through the clouds because Singapore was very interesting.

8 THE CINEMA

Mary likes the cinema very much. She has no lessons and no homework on Saturdays, so she always goes to the cinema that afternoon. She prefers funny films, but often she sees other kinds of films. She usually goes with some of her school-friends, and they all sit together and eat nuts and ice-cream and laugh when something funny happens. They are always very happy at the cinema.

Last Saturday Mary saw a film about a funny man. His name was Percy. Percy was fat and had a big, black moustache. He went out one night to play cards with his friends when his wife was asleep. When he was going home at midnight, a fierce dog ran after him and tore his trouser pocket, so Percy lost his key. He tried to climb up a ladder to get into his house through a window, but he slipped down the ladder and made a terrible noise. His wife woke up and cried, "Help! Thieves!" Someone telephoned to the police and a truck full of policemen arrived. Percy ran away, but he slipped and fell into the mud at the side of the river. Mary and her friends laughed a lot.

QUESTIONS

1 Put one word from this story in each empty place in these sentences:
a Mary does not go to school on ....
b Mary likes .... films more than other kinds.
c Percy's friends played .... with him.
d Percy lost his key because a .... tore his pocket.
e The police came to Percy's house in a ....

2 Find words in this story which mean about the same as:
(a) a lot (b) likes best (c) glad (d) shouted (e) with each other.

3 Choose the right sentence from (a), the right sentence from (b), etc.
a Mary goes to the cinema on Saturday afternoons.
Mary goes to the cinema every afternoon.
Mary always goes to the cinema when she has no lessons and no homework.
b Mary does not sit with her friends.
Mary always sits with her friends.
Mary usually sits with her friends.
c Percy's friends played cards with his wife.
Percy's friends played cards with him.
Percy played cards with his friend's wife.
d Percy wanted to get into his house.
Percy wanted to get into his friend's house.
Percy wanted to get his key.
e Percy ran away from the police.
Percy ran away from the thieves.
Percy ran away from his wife.

9 IN A BOAT

My family like the sea very much. When we have a holiday, we go to a place at the seaside and borrow a boat from one of our friends. Then we row, sail and fish on the sea all day. Sometimes we have races against other boats.

When the sea is rough, we row and sail on a small lake near the sea instead. We are very careful on this lake because there are a lot of sharp rocks there, and the water is shallow. We do not want to damage our friend's boat.

There are not many fish in the lake, but in the sea we sometimes catch a lot with a hook, line and small pieces of bread. The fish are not very big, but they taste very good. When the weather is fine, we row to the land at lunch time, collect pieces of dry wood and fry or grill our fish over them on the beach.

There is an island about a mile from our friend's house, and we often row or sail to it. The water is very clean there, and there is a beautiful beach with white sand and no rocks. We often bathe there.

QUESTIONS

1 Put one word from this story in each empty place in these sentences:
a We go to the sea because we .... it.
b A friend lends my family a ....
c The lake has a lot of .... in it.
d We put .... on our hooks and catch fish with it.
e We cook our fish over ....

2 Find words in the story which mean the opposite of:
(a) lend (b) smooth (c) deep (d) cloudy (e) dirty.

3 Choose the right sentence from (a), the right sentence from (b), etc.
a We row and sail every day.
  We row and sail on holidays.
  We row and sail only when the sea is rough.
b The sharp rocks do not damage the boat because we are careful.
  The sharp rocks do not damage the boat because we do not row on the lake.
  The sharp rocks sometimes damage the boat.
c There are a lot of big fish in the sea here.
  There are not many fish in the sea here.
  There are a lot of small fish in the sea here.
d We cook the fish on land.
  We cook the fish in the boat.
  We cook the fish on the rocks.
e We often go to our friend's house and bathe there.
  We often go to the island and bathe there.
  We often go to the rocks and bathe there.

10 MY UNCLE'S FARM

My uncle Tom has a small farm. He has a lot of chickens there. He sells eggs and chickens. Every summer, during the holidays, I go to his farm and help him. I feed the chickens and collect and clean the eggs. It is very interesting, and Uncle Tom pays me something for my help.

Twice a week we put the eggs in boxes and take them to town. There my uncle sells them. He gets quite a lot of money for them. Then he sometimes buys food for the chickens. He buys it in big bags because that is cheaper.

My uncle's hens are rather stupid and noisy, I think. They are very useful because they lay the eggs, but I don't like them very much. I prefer the baby chickens and the cocks.

My uncle has some white ducks too. They live on a pond on his farm. There is a low wall round the pond, with a small gate in it. Every evening my uncle puts a tin of food near the gate, and the ducks come up out of the pond to eat it. Then my uncle shuts the gate, and the ducks eat their food and go into their box. They sleep there at night.

QUESTIONS

1 Put one word from this story in each empty place in these sentences:
a I help my uncle when I have my summer ....
b My uncle gives me some .... for my help.
c I like the baby chickens and the cocks more than the ....
d The wall round the pond is ....
e The ducks eat their food from a ....

2 Find words in this story which mean almost the same as:
   (a) little (b) less expensive (c) also (d) not clever (e) close.

3 Choose the right sentence from (a), the right sentence from (b), etc.
a I live with my uncle Tom.
  I visit my uncle Tom in the summer only.
  I always visit my uncle Tom when I have a holiday.
b My uncle gets quite a lot of money for his eggs.
  My uncle gets quite a lot of money for his boxes.
  My uncle gets quite a lot of money for his chickens.
c I like baby chickens more than cocks.
  I like baby chickens more than hens.
  I like hens more than cocks.
d There is a small gate in the wall of the pond.
  There is a small gate in the pond.
  There is a small gate in the ducks' box.
e The ducks sleep by the gate.
  The ducks sleep on the pond.
  The ducks sleep in a box.

11 COWS

One of my friends (his name is Jim) has a farm. He has a lot of cows and sells their milk. He does not milk the cows by hand: he has an electric milking-machine. He gets up very early every morning, milks the cows with his machine, lets them out into the fields, gets the milk ready, puts it in very big cans, washes the milking-machine and the buckets, puts the milk-cans out in the road, and then has his breakfast. At about 8 o'clock a big truck comes and collects his milk-cans. It also collects milk from other farms.

After breakfast, Jim goes to his desk and writes letters and accounts and other things. When I visited him last year, he said to me, "Do you know, Bill, a farmer has a lot of paper-work now. He is like a clerk in an office." Jim loves his farm, but he hates paper-work.

After he has finished it, he cleans his cow-sheds and then goes out into his fields to look at his cows, or he cuts some grass, or does some work in his vegetable garden. He is always very busy, and his wife is too.

QUESTIONS

1 Put one word from this story in each empty place in these sentences:
a Jim's cows live on a ………. .
b A ………. milks the cows.
c Jim puts his milk in ………. , and then a truck collects them.
d My name is ………. .
e Jim's wife is a ………. woman.

2 Find words in this story which mean the opposite of:
(a) late (b) after (c) loves (d) begun (e) never has any work
(five words)

3 Choose the right sentence from (a), the right sentence from (b), etc.
a Jim milks the cows, and then they go out into the road.
Jim milks his cows, and then they go out into the fields.
Jim milks his cows, and then they go in a big truck.
b Jim milks his cows by electricity.
Jim milks his cows by hand.
Jim does not milk his cows.
c A big truck takes Jim's milk to other farms.
A big truck collects *Jim's* milk-cans only.
A big truck collects milk from Jim's farm and from other farms.
d Jim hates writing letters and accounts.
Jim loves writing letters and accounts.
Jim never writes letters or accounts.
e Jim's wife is lazy.
Jim's wife does some work in the vegetable garden.
Jim's wife has a lot of work.

12 FISHING

Henry likes fishing. He fishes in the river near our house. In the evenings he makes "flies" out of little pieces of wool and cotton and ties them to his hooks. Then on Saturday afternoon, when he has no work, he goes down to the river with a little seat and some sandwiches and fishes until it is quite dark. There are always a few other people there. They love fishing too, and they all sit there quietly for hours. Sometimes they catch some fish, sometimes they do not. I do not like that kind of sport, because I am not very patient.

Once Henry caught a big fish. He was very happy! All the other fishermen left their places and came to see his fish. One of them had a camera, so he took a photograph of Henry and his big fish. We still have the photograph on the wall of our living-room.

Another time Henry fell into the river! The grass was slippery because there was some mud on it, and while he was pulling his line in, he slipped and fell into the dirty water. Henry does not swim, but the two nearest fishermen pulled him out quickly, and he ran home, with mud all over his face!

QUESTIONS

1 Put one word from this story in each empty place in these sentences:
a Henry ties .... to his hooks.
b He sits on a .... when he is fishing.
c Henry is more .... than I am.
d When Henry fell into the river, he became ....
e When he got home, there was mud on his ....

2 Find words in this story which mean about the same as:
(a) like very much (b) with no noise (c) pleased (d) went away from (e) to his house.

3 Choose the right sentence from (a), the right sentence from (b), etc.
a Henry puts sandwiches on his hooks.
  Henry puts "flies" on his hooks.
  Henry puts ties on his hooks.
b Henry fishes with other people.
  Henry fishes with me.
  Henry fishes alone.
c I do not like fishing.
  I do not like sport.
  I am not kind.
d Henry photographed the big fish.
  We photographed the big fish.
  Another fisherman photographed the big fish.
e Henry fell because the water was dirty.
  Henry fell because there was some mud on his line.
  Henry fell because the grass was slippery.

13 PHOTOGRAPHS

Have you got a camera? I have got a good one. I like taking photographs. It is my hobby. I prefer colour photographs because they are more beautiful than black and white ones. I usually have a colour film in my camera. I like photographing flowers very much. I have some very good photographs of the roses in my garden. I also like photographing children. I watch them carefully and wait patiently until I get a good picture of them. It is not easy, because children move very quickly and they never stop except when they are asleep.

Some of my friends like to show all their photographs to others. They invite them to dinner and then bring out their photographs. Some of them are terrible (... "And here is a photograph of an old man and a donkey. I took it in Italy last summer. It was rather dark when I took it, and the donkey was half behind a rock, but its tail is there—on the left. Do you see it? ... Yes, that thing on the right is the old man's back. He turned round before I took the photograph" ...). *I* show my photographs only when people want to see them; and I show only my *good* ones!

QUESTIONS

1 Put one word from this story in each empty place in these sentences:
 a I like .... photographs more than black and white ones.
 b I like taking .... of flowers and children.
 c Some people bring out their photographs after ....
 d The donkey's .... is in the photograph.
 e I never .... my bad photographs to my friends.

2 Find words in this story which mean the opposite of:
 (a) ugly (b) hard (c) slowly (d) awake (e) next.

3 Choose the right sentence from (a), the right sentence from (b), etc.
 a I prefer photographing flowers and children.
   I prefer photographing colours.
   I prefer photographing people.
 b Photographing children is difficult because they go to sleep.
   Photographing children is not difficult.
   Photographing children is difficult because they are always moving.
 c Some of my friends' photographs are terrible.
   Some of my friends are terrible.
   Some of my photographs are terrible.
 d You don't see all of the donkey in the photograph because it is rather dark.
   You don't see all of the donkey in the photograph because there is a rock in front of it.
   You don't see all of the donkey because its tail is behind a rock.
 e The old man took a photograph.
   The old man turned round.
   The old man came back.

14 THE BATTLE

It is a hot day. We are quite near the cool, blue sea, but our soldiers are waiting for an attack. The enemy are only half a mile away. Their aeroplanes are dropping bombs on us every quarter of an hour. They come down with the sun behind them, and when we try to shoot at them, the sun shines in our eyes and makes it difficult. Our air force has lost all its aeroplanes, so no aeroplanes attack the enemy ones. One bomb killed our captain this morning, and another killed three of our soldiers.

We are on a narrow piece of flat land, with the sea and the beach on our right, and a steep, rough mountain on the other side. The enemy are behind a low hill. It goes down almost to the sea half a mile from here. They tried to attack when they got to that hill yesterday afternoon, but our guns were ready for them and drove them back. Three of their tanks caught fire and burned for a long time.

During the night and this morning the enemy brought up more and more guns and tanks and soldiers. They will attack again soon.

QUESTIONS

1 Put one word from this story in each empty place in these sentences:
a The enemy are going to .... us soon.
b The sun makes it difficult to .... at the enemy aeroplanes.
c Our soldiers are between the sea and a ....
d Our .... drove the enemy back.
e The enemy .... burned for a long time.

2 Find words in this story which mean the opposite of:
(a) warm (b) easy (c) wide (d) smooth (e) less.

3 Choose the right sentence from (a), the right sentence from (b), etc.
a Our soldiers are not bathing because the sea is cool.
Our soldiers are not bathing because they are waiting for an attack.
Our soldiers are bathing in the sea.
b It is difficult to shoot at the enemy aeroplanes because the sun shines in our eyes.
It is difficult to shoot at the enemy aeroplanes because they come down behind us.
It is not difficult to shoot at the enemy aeroplanes.
c No other aeroplanes shoot at the enemy ones because we have no air force.
No other aeroplanes shoot at the enemy ones because we have no aeroplanes.
No other aeroplanes shoot at the enemy ones because a bomb killed our captain.
d The enemy drove our soldiers back yesterday afternoon.
The enemy drove our guns back yesterday afternoon.
Our soldiers drove the enemy back yesterday afternoon.
e We are between the sea and a mountain.
We are between flat land and a mountain.
We are between the sea and the beach.

15 SNOW!

Have you ever seen snow? A lot of people in the world have not. A lot of countries never have snow—or they have it only on the tops of very high mountains. In Scotland and in the north of England, there is quite a lot of snow every winter, but in the south of England, there is usually little.

When a student from a warm country like Malaya or Indonesia comes to Britain in the autumn for the first time, he feels cold at first. There are often dark clouds, grey sky and cold rain in Britain in autumn, and most students from warm countries do not like this.

But snow is different. Although it is very cold, it is also very beautiful. Perhaps, after several dark mornings, the student wakes up one day, and there is a lot of light in his room. He thinks, "Is it so late?" and jumps out of bed. But no, it is not very late. He looks out of the window—and there is the snow, on the ground and on the roofs of the houses and everywhere. The light in his room came from that smooth, clean, beautiful white snow.

QUESTIONS

1 Put one word from this story in each empty place in these sentences:
a A lot of people have never seen ....
b There is less snow in the .... of England than in Scotland.
c Most students from warm countries do not like the weather in Britain in .... at first.
d The student's room is not .... when there is snow on the ground.
e The student sees snow ....

2 Find words in this story which mean almost the same as:
(a) tall (b) not much (c) not the same (d) in all places (e) not dirty.

3 Choose the right sentence from (a), the right sentence from (b), etc.
a A lot of people have never seen snow.
  A lot of people have not seen much snow.
  There are not many people in the world.
b There is usually more snow in Scotland than in the north of England.
  There is usually more snow in the north of England than in the south.
  There is usually more snow in the south of England than in Scotland.
c Most students from warm countries do not like Britain.
  Most students from warm countries do not like snow.
  Most students from warm countries do not like grey sky.
d There is a lot of light in the student's room because there is snow everywhere.
  There is a lot of light in the student's room because it is early.
  There is a lot of light in the student's room because it is late.
e The snow is beautiful.
  The light in the student's room is beautiful.
  The student's room is beautiful.

16 THE FOOTBALL MATCH

My brother Fred and I went to a football match yesterday. Our school team was playing against the High School team. Our team wore red and white shirts, white shorts and red stockings. The other team wore orange and black shirts, black shorts and orange stockings. "They look like bees," my brother said, and we laughed.

They played like bees too. They ran very fast, attacked very hard and passed the ball to each other very fast. Soon they scored their first goal. Fred and I shouted and shouted, "Come on, Valley School! Come on, the Valleys!" Our headmaster was near us and he was shouting too. But the High School scored another goal. We were very sad!

Then one of the "bees" stopped the ball with one of his hands, so our team got a free kick. Our captain took it—and scored a goal. We shouted, "Hooray!" The score was now two : one. That was better!

Now our team began to play better—or the "bees" were getting tired. Our team scored another goal before half-time.

In the second half of the match, both teams tried very hard, but neither scored, so at the end the score was still two all.

QUESTIONS

1 Put one word from this story in each empty place in these sentences:
a My brother and I go to the .... School.
b The "bees" wore .... stockings.
c Our captain took the ....
d Our team .... two goals.
e .... team won the football match.

2 Find words in this story which mean about the same as:
(a) quickly (b) strongly (c) cried (d) started (e) becoming.

3 Choose the right sentence from (a), the right sentence from (b), etc.
a The High School team had white shorts.
  The High School team had black shorts.
  The High School team had orange and black shorts.
b My brother said, "They look like bees" because they ran very fast.
  My brother said, "They look like bees" because they had orange and black clothes.
  My brother said, "They look like bees" because we laughed.
c The High School team scored first.
  The Valley School team scored first.
  Fred scored the first goal.
d Our team got a free kick because our captain took it.
  Our team got a free kick because the "bees" were getting tired.
  Our team got a free kick because a High School boy stopped the ball with one of his hands.
e We won the match.
  Neither team won the match.
  The "bees" won the match.

17 THE THIEF

Yesterday my mother went into a shop to buy some fruit and vegetables. She put her basket and her handbag down on a table and went to look at some apples in the window. There were a lot of people in the shop. When the shopkeeper was free, he weighed a pound of apples for my mother, put them in a paper-bag and said, "That will be one shilling and fourpence, Mrs Jones."

My mother said, "My money is in my handbag on that table." She went to the table—but the handbag was not there! The basket was on the table, but the handbag was not! My mother was very surprised.

Suddenly there was a lot of noise at the door of the shop, and a policeman came in. He was holding a man and my mother's bag. "Has anybody here lost a handbag?" the policeman asked. "Yes," my mother answered. "That's mine." The policeman looked in the bag and said, "How much money did you have?" "Two pounds, three shillings and a few pennies," my mother said. "It is all here," the policeman said and gave her her bag. "I caught the thief outside. He was running away."

My mother was lucky, wasn't she?

QUESTIONS

1 Put one word from this story in each empty place in these sentences:
a My mother's money was in her ....
b The .... cost one shilling and fourpence.
c A .... took my mother's bag.
d A .... brought my mother's bag back.
e .... my mother's money was still in her bag.

2 Find words in this story which mean the opposite of:
(a) sell (b) a few (c) busy (d) found (e) inside.

3 Choose the right sentence from (a), the right sentence from (b), etc.
a Mrs Jones had one shilling and fourpence when she came into the shop.
Mrs Jones had no money when she came into the shop.
Mrs Jones had more than two pounds when she came into the shop.
b The thief took my mother's handbag off a table.
The thief took my mother's basket off a table.
The thief took my mother's basket and handbag off a table.
c The shopkeeper's name was Jones.
My mother's name is Jones.
The thief's name was Jones.
d The policeman caught the thief at the door of the shop.
The policeman caught the thief by the table.
The policeman caught the thief in the street.

18 OUR PLAYGROUND

In our town we have got a big park. It has lots of trees and flowers and grass and benches in it, and there are places for tennis and volley-ball and a small restaurant. There is also a pond for small boats and a very small zoo, with a few wild animals in it.

But, for children, the best place in the park is the playground. There they can swing and slide and go round and round for hours. During school hours, only the very small children are there, but on summer evenings and on Saturdays and Sundays all the year, there are older children too.

I like going to the playground with my children because all the children are happy there. They laugh and shout and joke with each other, and although sometimes one of them falls down and hurts his knees (usually it is a boy!), he soon gets up again and stops crying and begins to play with his friends again.

There is a shed near the playground, and when it rains hard, the children go in there and wait until the rain stops. Then they come out again, running and shouting and laughing, and in a minute they are all sliding and swinging and going round and round again.

QUESTIONS

1 Put one word from this story in each empty place in these sentences:
a The playground is in the ....
b The animals are in the ....
c The .... children do not come to the playground during school hours.
d The children are very .... in the playground.
e The children go into a .... when it rains.

2 Find words in this story which have about the same meaning as: (*a*) seats (*b*) small lake (*c*) slip (*d*) starts (*e*) heavily.

3 Choose the right sentence from (*a*), the right sentence from (*b*), etc.
a The zoo is in a pond.
   The zoo is in the playground.
   The zoo is in our park.
b The very small children go to the playground during school hours only.
   The very small children go to the playground on summer evenings and on Saturdays and Sundays all the year.
   The very small children go to the playground both during school hours and at other times.
c More boys than girls hurt their knees.
   More girls than boys hurt their knees.
   People hurt boys more than girls.
d When a child falls down in the playground, it does not stop crying.
   When a child falls down in the playground, it does not cry for long.
   When a child falls down in the playground, it does not cry.
e The children play in a shed near the playground when the rain stops.
   The children go into a shed near the playground when there is heavy rain.
   The children stay in the playground when it rains hard.

19 HOBBIES

My hobby is collecting stamps. When I began, I collected the stamps of all countries, but there are too many, so now I collect only Greek and Indian ones, because I have friends in Greece, and I live in India. Some of my stamps are very pretty, and they are all interesting. When you look at stamps carefully, they teach you a lot about the history of their country.

My small brother's hobby is watching trains. He goes to our station and watches them there. When an engine goes through the station, he writes down its name and number. He likes train-watching very much, but I don't. I went to the station with him one day, but it wasn't interesting, I thought.

My big sister's hobby is sewing. She hasn't got a sewing-machine, but she sews with our mother's. Sometimes she sews by hand, too. She makes most of her clothes, and when I tear my shirt or my trousers, I take them to her and she mends them.

My father has a hobby too. It is gardening. Every Saturday and Sunday afternoon, and sometimes on other summer evenings too, he digs, or plants flowers, or cuts the thick grass.

QUESTIONS

1 Put one word from this story in each empty place in these sentences:
a All my stamps are ....
b You learn about .... from stamps.
c I don't like ....
d My mother has a ....
e My sister sometimes .... my shirts.

2 Find words in this story which have about the same meaning as:
(a) started (b) a lot (c) also (d) damage (e) not thin.

3 Choose the right sentence from (a), the right sentence from (b), etc.
a I do not collect the stamps of all countries because I have friends in Greece and I live in India.
  I do not collect the stamps of all countries because there are too many.
  I collect the stamps of all countries.
b My brother writes down the names and numbers of stations.
  My brother writes down the names and numbers of engines.
  My brother writes down the names and numbers of trains.
c I do not like train-watching.
  I like train-watching.
  I don't like my brother.
d My sister mends most of her clothes.
  My sister makes our mother's clothes.
  My sister mends my clothes.
e My father works in the garden because he has plants and flowers.
  My father works in the garden because the summer evenings are very long.
  My father works in the garden because it is his hobby.

20 IN THE KITCHEN

I learned to cook when I was at school. We had lessons twice a week. Sometimes we made a mistake and burned the food; but usually we cooked it nicely and then ate it. I passed a cooking examination last year.

But I learned more about cooking at home, from my mother, than at school, from my teacher, because I often helped my mother in the kitchen, and sometimes I cooked a meal alone.

We have a gas stove in our kitchen, and it is quite easy to cook on it, and to bake things in its oven. I make chocolate cake best, my mother says. I put flour, butter, sugar, eggs and chocolate in it. I mix them well in a bowl and then put them in a baking-tin. Then I put the tin in the oven and bake it for one and a half hours.

I also make jam. In summer and autumn, when fruit is cheap, we buy a lot of it, and I boil it with sugar. Then I put it in pots and put the pots in a cupboard. In winter and spring, when there is not much fruit and it is expensive, our jam is very useful.

QUESTIONS

1 Put one word from this story in each empty place in these sentences:
a Our stove works by ....
b You bake cakes in an ....
c There are .... in a chocolate cake.
d You make jam out of .... and ....

2 Find words in this story which mean about the same as:
(*a*) two times (*b*) breakfast, or lunch, or dinner, or supper
(*c*) without help (*d*) not expensive (*e*) a lot of.

3 Choose the right sentence from (*a*), the right sentence from (*b*), etc.
a My teacher and my mother taught me to cook.
Only my teacher taught me to cook.
Only my mother taught me to cook.
b My mother always cooked with me at home.
My mother never cooked with me at home.
My mother sometimes cooked with me at home.
c It is not difficult to bake in our oven.
It is not easy to bake in our oven.
We do not bake things in our oven.
d I boil jam in pots.
I boil jam with sugar.
I bake jam in our oven.
e Fruit is cheap in winter and spring.
Fruit is expensive in summer and autumn.
Fruit is expensive in winter and spring.

21 A PARTY

We are going to have a party in our house this evening. It is my mother's birthday, and she has invited my uncles and aunts and some of her friends. Mother and I are cooking most of the food for the party, and Father is getting the drinks. The living-room looks very pretty. Balloons of all colours are hanging from the lights, and we have taken the carpets away because we are going to dance there after dinner.

In the dining-room we have put out the best plates and glasses and table-cloths, and it all looks beautiful. We are going to have soup, fish, chicken, fruit and cheese. We are going to dance until midnight, and after that, we will have some more food, because we will be hungry after all that dancing.

Last year my mother had her birthday-party in a restaurant, but it is pleasanter (and cheaper!) at home.

When it is my birthday (it is in June), I am going to invite my friends and have a party in the garden. (It never rains here in June.) I will hang pretty lights in the trees, and we will grill our food in the garden and dance on the grass.

QUESTIONS

1 Put one word from this story in each empty place in these sentences:
a My mother is having a birthday- .... today.
b We are not going to dance on the ....
c We are going to stop dancing at .... and then have some food.
d My mother's birthday-party was in a .... last year.
e We are going to eat and dance in the .... at my party.

2 Find words in this story which mean the opposite of:
(*a*) worst (*b*) before (*c*) next (*d*) more expensive (*e*) ugly.

3 Choose the right sentence from (*a*), the right sentence from (*b*), etc.
a My mother has her birthday-party in our house every year.
My mother has her birthday-party in my uncle's and aunt's house.
My mother sometimes has her birthday-party in our house.
b We are going to dance on the carpets after dinner.
We are going to dance in the living-room after dinner.
We are going away after dinner.
c We are going to eat only before our dance.
We are going to eat only after our dance.
We are going to eat before and after our dance.
d A birthday-party is more expensive in a restaurant than at home.
A birthday-party is cheaper in a restaurant than at home.
A birthday-party is pleasanter in a restaurant than at home.
e My name is June.
My birthday is in June.
It is June now.

22 AT THE BARBER'S

I go to the barber every three weeks. I don't like very short hair, so my barber doesn't cut off much. I have known him for almost four years now, and when I go to him, we always talk a lot. He tells me all his news, and I tell him all mine. He meets a lot of interesting people in his shop and he talks to most of them, so he always has a lot of news for me.

Every year my barber goes to France for two weeks for his holidays, and when he comes back to England, he has a lot of interesting news. While he is cutting my hair, he tells me about beautiful old cities and quiet little villages, strange food and drinks and many other things. I sit there and listen to the old man with open ears. One minute, my barber's chair is a seat in a French train, and the next minute it becomes a chair in a restaurant in Amiens.

Although my barber is old, he always tries new things. He never says, "I have never eaten this food before, so I am not going to eat it now." He says instead, "Try everything once."

QUESTIONS

1 Put one word from this story in each empty place in these sentences:
a My barber does not cut my hair very ....
b I always give my barber all my ....
c My barber .... goes to France for his holidays.
d My barber drinks .... drinks in France.
e My barber is always ready to try .... things.

2 Find words in this story which mean the opposite of:
 (*a*) long (*b*) few (*c*) noisy (*d*) young (*e*) never.

3 Choose the right sentence from (*a*), the right sentence from (*b*), etc.
a The barber cuts my hair very short.
 The barber leaves my hair rather long.
 The barber doesn't cut my hair.
b My barber gets his news from a lot of people.
 My barber gets all his news from France.
 My barber gets all his news from me.
c My barber works in France.
 My barber works in Amiens.
 My barber works in England.
d I go to a restaurant in Amiens with my barber.
 My barber tells me about a restaurant in Amiens.
 My barber cuts my hair in a French train.
e My barber tastes all new food.
 My barber never eats new food.
 My barber has never eaten French food.

23 AT THE DENTIST'S

I go to the dentist every six months. I don't like going to him, but I have got good, white teeth, and I don't want to lose any of them. I telephoned my dentist two weeks ago, and last Tuesday I went to see him.

His nurse said, "Good morning, Miss Robinson. Will you please wait in the waiting-room?" I went in and sat down. There are always a lot of magazines there, so I took one and began reading an interesting story. After a few minutes, the nurse came in and said, "Mr Williams will see you now, Miss Robinson." "I will finish this story next time," I thought, because I usually come back two or three times.

The dentist is always very kind. He tries not to hurt me, but sometimes he does, and then he says, "It will soon be finished, Miss Robinson. Be patient," and gives me a pleasant smile.

This time, Mr Williams looked at all my teeth very carefully and then said, "Your teeth are quite all right this time, Miss Robinson." I was very glad, but I said, "Oh, now I won't finish that story in the magazine in your waiting-room!" Mr Williams laughed, and I did too.

QUESTIONS

1 Put one word from this story in each empty place in these sentences:
 a My name is ....
 b I visit my dentist .... a year.
 c When I go to my dentist's house, I wait in his ....
 d I read an interesting story in a ....
 e Mr Williams is a ....

2 Find words in this story which mean the opposite of:
 (a) stood up (b) begin (c) nasty (d) carelessly (e) sad.

3 Choose the right sentence from (a), the right sentence from (b), etc.
 a I go to the dentist every six months because I like going to him.
   I go to the dentist every six months because I don't want to lose any of my teeth.
   I go to the dentist every six months because I have good teeth.
 b I waited in the waiting-room.
   The nurse waited for me in the waiting-room.
   The dentist waited for me in the waiting-room.
 c I read the story in the magazine two or three times.
   I finished the story in the magazine the next time.
   I did not finish the story in the magazine.
 d Mr Williams sometimes hurts me.
   Mr Williams does not hurt me.
   Mr Williams always hurts me.
 e I was very glad because Mr Williams smiled.
   I was very glad because my teeth were all right.
   I was very glad because Mr Williams looked at my teeth carefully.

24 AN ACCIDENT

John was driving home from the station in his car yesterday evening when he had an accident. He was driving along a main road at about 30 miles an hour when another car came out of a side road and hit his. There was a lot of damage to both cars, and both John and the other man were hurt. One of John's arms was broken, and the other man had a bad cut on his head.

Another car was following John's. It stopped quickly and a man and a woman got out of it. They ran to the damaged cars and pulled John and the other man out of them because they thought, "Perhaps the petrol in these cars will catch fire and burn the two men."

The man and the woman had some cotton-wool and bandages in their car, so they put them on the cuts on John's arm and on the other man's head. Then they telephoned a doctor and the police. Soon an ambulance arrived and took the two men to hospital. Then two policemen arrived too and began to measure things. A truck came and pulled the two cars off the road.

QUESTIONS

1 Put one word from this story in each empty place in these sentences:
a John's car was on a .... road.
b The other man's car was on a .... road.
c John's car was ....
d The man and the woman .... to John's car and the other man's car.
e John and the other man went to hospital in an ....

2 Find words in this story which mean the opposite of:
(*a*) in front of   (*b*) slowly   (*c*) pushed   (*d*) finished   (*e*) on.

3 Choose the right sentence from (*a*), the right sentence from (*b*), etc.
a John's car hit another one.
Another car hit John's.
A car hit John.
b A man and a woman got out of John's car.
A man and a woman got out of their car.
A man and a woman got out of the damaged cars.
c The petrol did not burn the two men.
The fire burned the two men.
The petrol burned the two men.
d The man and the woman took John and the other man to hospital.
The ambulance took John and the other man to hospital.
The policemen took John and the other man to hospital.
e Two cars pulled the police truck off the road.
A truck pulled two police cars off the road.
A truck pulled John's car off the road.

25 IN HOSPITAL

After the accident, an ambulance took John to hospital. Then two men carried him to a bed and put him in it carefully. A nurse came and wrote his name and address in a book. She gave him some tea to drink, and then the doctor came. He took the bandage off John's arm, looked at it carefully and put his hands on it. "Yes, it is broken," he said. "We will do something about it this afternoon. It won't hurt you. We will give you an injection, and you won't feel anything. You will be all right soon." "Thank you, doctor," John said.

John was in hospital for a week. The nurses were very kind. The first night, his arm hurt a lot, but a nurse gave him another injection, and he went to sleep and slept until the morning.

The next afternoon, his father and mother came to visit him. They brought him some flowers and fruit and magazines. He was very glad to see them. There were several other men in John's room in the hospital. John talked with them, listened to the radio, read his magazines and slept, and the days passed, until the week ended and he went home again.

QUESTIONS

1 Put one word from this story in each empty place in these sentences:
a John went to hospital in an ....
b John had a .... round his arm.
c John went to sleep after he had his ....
d John's father and mother .... him some presents.
e John talked with the .... men in his room.

2 Find words in this story which mean about the same as:
(*a*) car for carrying sick people   (*b*) give pain   (*c*) after a short time   (*d*) pleased   (*e*) more than one.

3 Choose the right sentence from (*a*), the right sentence from (*b*), etc.
a John went to hospital because he had an accident.
   John went to hospital because he was in an ambulance.
   John went to hospital because two men carried him.
b A nurse wrote the two men's names in a book.
   A nurse wrote John's name in a book.
   John wrote the nurse's name and address in a book.
c John's hands were broken.
   The doctor's arm was broken.
   John's arm was broken.
d A nurse gave John an injection because she was very kind.
   A nurse gave John an injection because his arm hurt.
   A nurse gave John an injection because he went to sleep.
e John was in a room with some other men in the hospital.
   John was in a room with his father and mother only in the hospital.
   John was alone in a room in the hospital.

26 IN THE OFFICE

Jean works in an office. Five days in the week, she gets up very early in the morning, has a quick breakfast, and then walks to Finsbury Park station. From there she goes to King's Cross station in London by train. Then she gets in a bus and goes to her office in Holborn. There she works as a typist. She types letters and accounts and other things for Mr James. Jean likes her work and she likes the other people in her office. There are three other typists and three clerks. There is also an office-boy. His name is Joe, and he takes the letters to the post-office, makes the tea and does other things like that.

At lunch time, Jean goes to a small restaurant near the office, and sometimes she also goes to the shops, either to buy something, or only to look at the things in the shop-windows. She likes pretty clothes very much.

At 5.30 p.m. Jean's office closes, and she goes home, first by bus to King's Cross station again, then to Finsbury Park station by train, and then on foot to her house. She lives with her parents. They are quite old.

Jean does not work on Saturday and Sunday. She usually stays at home on those days.

QUESTIONS

1 Put one word from this story in each empty place in these sentences:
a Jean goes from King's Cross station to Holborn by ....
b There are four .... in Jean's office.
c The .... makes the tea in Jean's office.
d Jean has her lunch in a ....
e Jean's parents are .... people.

2 Find words in this story which mean about the same as:
(*a*) out of bed (*b*) person who types (*c*) shuts (*d*) walking (*e*) mother and father.

3 Choose the right sentence from (*a*), the right sentence from (*b*), etc.
a Jean gets up early on Saturday and Sunday.
  Jean gets up early every day.
  Jean gets up early on Monday, Tuesday, Wednesday, Thursday and Friday.
b Jean goes from her home to her office by bus.
  Jean goes from her home to her office on foot.
  Jean goes from her home to her office on foot, by train and by bus.
c Jean works for Mr James.
  Jean works for the typists.
  Jean works for the other people in the office.
d Jean goes home with her parents.
  Jean goes home at half past five.
  Jean goes home at a quarter past five.
e Jean never goes out on Saturday and Sunday.
  Jean seldom goes out on Saturday and Sunday.
  Jean usually goes out on Saturday and Sunday

27 CYCLING

David likes cycling very much. He belongs to a cycling club, and almost every Saturday afternoon, he goes off on his bicycle with his friends. In summer he takes his little tent and his stove with him, and camps in some beautiful place in the country. When it rains, it is not very pleasant, but when the sun shines and the weather is warm, camping is very nice. David and his friends cook their meal on their little stoves, make a fire and then sing round it until it is almost midnight. Then they get under their blankets in their little tents and go to sleep.

Sometimes there are bicycle races, and David goes to see them. They are very interesting. Sometimes David's big brother George rides in these races. Once he won a race and got a beautiful silver cup. David was very happy.

David wants to take his bicycle to Germany next summer. He will go from England to Belgium by ship and then ride to Cologne on his bicycle. He will go with some of his friends from the cycling club. They will camp every night. Cycling and camping are quite cheap, and David's father will give him money for the ship. He will have a very good time, I think.

QUESTIONS

1 Put one word from this story in each empty place in these sentences:
a David's hobby is ....
b When David is camping, he cooks his food over his ....
c David sleeps in a .... when he is camping.
d David is George's ....
e .... and .... do not cost very much.

2 You will find the names of these things in this story. What are they?

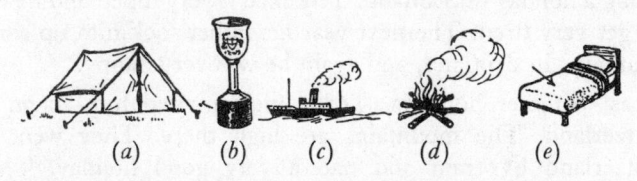

(*a*)   (*b*)   (*c*)   (*d*)   (*e*)

3 Choose the right sentence from (*a*), the right sentence from (*b*), etc.
a David and his friends cycle on nearly all Saturdays in summer only.
David and his friends cycle on nearly all Saturdays in the year.
David and his friends cycle on all Saturdays in the year.
b David and his friends camp when the sun shines.
David and his friends camp in summer.
David and his friends camp almost every Saturday.
c David and his friends cook their food when it is almost midnight.
David and his friends cook their food at midnight.
David and his friends cook their food at night.
d George won a bicycle race.
David won a bicycle race.
One of David's friends won a bicycle race.
e David's holiday in Germany will not cost him much because he will go by ship.
David's holiday in Germany will not cost him much because cycling and camping are cheap.
David's holiday in Germany will not cost him much because his father will give him money for it all.

28 CLIMBING MOUNTAINS

Do you like climbing mountains? My friend Ted does. He has never climbed a dangerous mountain, but he has climbed some quite big and difficult ones. He began to climb rocks when he was quite a small boy. Then his father took him with him one summer when he climbed some hills while the family were having a holiday in Scotland. Ted liked it very much and he did not get very tired. The next year his father took him up some mountains in Scotland, and again he was very happy.

Last summer holidays, Ted's uncle invited him to go to Switzerland. The mountains are high there. They went to Switzerland by train and had a very good holiday. They climbed several mountains. Once Ted's uncle tied him to him with a rope because the mountain was rather steep. At the end of the holidays he said to Ted, "You are still very young, but you already climb well." Ted was very glad.

Now Ted wants to go to India to climb some of the very high mountains in the Himalayas, but he is still too young, and also he hasn't got enough money. Perhaps one day he will become rich, and then he will go to India.

QUESTIONS

1 Put one word from this story in each empty place in these sentences:
a Before Ted started to climb hills, he climbed ....
b Ted climbed some hills with his ....
c Ted's uncle tied him with a rope on a .... mountain.
d Now Ted wants to go to the .... to .... there.

2 Find words in this story which mean the opposite of:
(a) safe (b) easy (c) low (d) badly (e) sad.

3 Choose the right sentence from (a), the right sentence from (b), etc.
a Only Ted's father climbed the hills in Scotland.
  Only Ted's uncle climbed the hills in Scotland.
  Ted and his father climbed the hills in Scotland.
b Ted had climbed mountains in Scotland only.
  Ted has climbed mountains in Scotland and Switzerland only.
  Ted has climbed mountains in Scotland, Switzerland and India.
c Ted and his uncle had a holiday in Scotland.
  Ted and his uncle had a holiday in Switzerland.
  Ted and his uncle had a holiday in India.
d Ted's uncle tied him when he was on a rather steep mountain.
  Ted's uncle tied him when he was on a train in Switzerland.
  Ted's uncle tied him when he was on several high mountains.
e Ted has not gone to India yet because it is too expensive.
  Ted has not gone to India yet because the mountains are too high there.
  Ted has not gone to India yet because he is rich.

APPENDIX

A THOUSAND WORD VOCABULARY

(*Note:* This vocabulary does not contain numerals, names of the days of the week, names of the months or proper nouns and adjectives. Not all cases of nouns and pronouns are given (e.g. *boy* stands for *boy—boy's—boys—boys'*; *I* stands for *I—me—my—mine*); nor are all parts of verbs given (e.g. *swim* stands for *swim—swims—swam—swum—swimming*). Comparatives and superlatives of adjectives and adverbs are not given.

The abbreviation a. means adjective and/or adverb; n. means noun; and v. means verb.)

about
above
absent (*a.*)
accept
accident
account (*n.*)
ache
across
address (*n.*)
aeroplane
afraid
after
afternoon
again
against
ago
air force
air(*port*)
all
almost
alone
along
also
although
always
a.m.
ambulance
among
a(*n*)
and

angry
animal
answer
ant
any
apple
arm
army
around
arrive
artist
as
ask
asleep
at
attack
aunt
autumn
avoid
awake
away

baby
back (*a.*)
back (*n.*)
bad (*worse, worst*)
bag
bake
ball

balloon
banana
bandage
bank
bar
barber
bargain
basin
basket
bath
bathe
battle
be
beach
bean
bear (*n.*)
beard
beat (*v.*)
beautiful
because
become
bed
bee
before
begin(*ning*)
behind
bell
belong
belt
bench

besides
between
bicycle
big
bill
bird
birthday
bite
bitter
black
blackboard
blanket
blood
blouse
blow (*v.*)
blue
boat
body (and
 -body, e.g.
 in *anybody*)
boil (*v.*)
bomb
book
boot
born
borrow
both
bottle
bottom
bowl (*n.*)

box (*n.*)
boy
branch
brave
bread
break
breakfast
bridge
bright
bring
broken
brother
brown
brush
bucket
build(*ing*)
bunch
burn
burst
bus
bush
busy
but
butter
button
buy
by

cage
cake

camera
camp
can (*n.*)
canal
cap
captain
car
card
careful
careless
carpet
carriage
carry
cart
cat
catch
ceiling
chain
chair
chalk
change
cheap
cheek
cheese
chemist
chest
chicken
child
chimney
chin

chocolate	cross (n.)	drop	fat	game	hate
choose	cross (v.)	dry	father	garage	have
church	crowd(ed)	duck	feel	garden	he
cigarette	cry	during	fence	gas	head
cinema	cup	duster	few	gate	headmaster/
circle	cupboard	dust(y)	field	gentleman	mistress
city	curtain		fierce	get	hear
class	cut	each	fight	girl	heart
clean	cycle	ear	fill	give	heavy
clerk		early	film	glad	help
clever	damage(d)	earth	find	glass	hen
climate	damp	east	fine (a.)	glue	here
climb	dance	easy	finger	go	hide (v.)
clock	dangerous	eat	finish(ed)	goal	high
close (v.)	dark	egg	fire	goat	hill
cloth	date	either	first	God	history
clothes	daughter	electric(ity)	fish(erman)	good(better/	hit
cloud(y)	day	elephant	flag	best)	hobby
club	dead	else	flat	goodbye	hold
coat	deep	empty	floor	gramophone	hole
cock	dentist	end	flour	grand- (e.g.	holiday
coffee	desk	enemy	flower	in grand-	home(work)
cold	die	engine	fly (n.)	father)	honey
collar	different	enjoy	fly (v.)	grass	hook
collect	difficult	enough	follow	green	hooray
colour	dining(-room,	equal	food	grey	horse
comb	-hall)	evening	foot(ball)	grill	hospital
come	dinner	ever	for	ground	host(ess)
common	dirty	every(where)	foreign	group	hot
continue	discover	examination	forest	grow	hotel
cook	dish	except	forget	guest	hour
cool	dive	excuse	fork	gun	house
copy	do	exercise	forward		how
corn	doctor	expensive	free	hair	hullo
corner	dog	eye	fresh	half	hungry
correct	donkey		friend	hall	hurry
cost	door		frighten(ed)	hammer	hurt
cotton(-wool)	double	face	from	hand	husband
cough	down	factory	front	handkerchief	
count (v.)	draw	fall	fruit	hang	I
country	dream	family	fry	happen	ice(-cream)
course	dress	famous	full	happy	ill
cover(ed)	drink	far	funny	hard	important
cow	drive	fast	furniture	hat	injection

61

ink	leaf	marbles	nail	once	pink
inside	learn	marry	name	one(and -one	place
instead	least	mat	narrow	e.g. in any-	plant
interesting	leave	match	nasty	one)	plate
in(to)	left	mathematics	near	only	play(ground)
invite	leg	matter	necessary	open	pleasant
iron	lend	meal	neck	opposite	please(d)
island	less	mean (v.)	need	or	plough
it	lesson	measure	needle	orange	p.m.
	let	meat	neighbour	other	pocket
	letter	medicine	neither	out	poem
jam	lid	meet(ing)	nephew	outside	point (v.)
jar	lie (v.)	melt	nest	oven	poisonous
joke	light (a.)	mend	net	over	police(man)
journey	light (n. & v.)	midday	never	owe	pond
jug	like (a.)	middle	new		pool (e.g.
jump	like (v.)	midnight	news(paper)	page	swimming-
	line	mile	next	pain	pool)
	lion	milk	nice	paint	poor
keep	listen	mind	niece	paper	port
key	little	minute (n.)	night	parcel	post (-card,
kick	live (v.)	miss (v.)	no	parent	-man, office)
kill	living-room	Miss	noise (noisy)	park	pot
kind (a.)	loaf	mistake	none	party	potato
kind (n.)	lock(ed)	mix	nor	pass	pound
kitchen	long (a.)	model	north	passenger	pour
kite	look	money	nose	past	pray
kneel	lose	monkey	not	path	prefer
knife	lot	month	now	patient (a.)	present (a.)
knock	loud	moon	number	pay	present (n.)
know	love	more	nurse	pen	pretty
	lucky	morning	nut	pencil	price
ladder	luggage	mosque		penny	pull
lady	lump	most	o'clock	people	punctual
lake	lunch	mother	of	perhaps	pupil
lamp		mountain	off	person	push
land		mouse	offer	petrol	put
language	machine	moustache	office	photograph	
last	madam	mouth	officer	pick	
late	magazine	move	often	picnic	quarter
laugh	main	Mr(s)	oh	picture	question
lavatory	make	much	oil	piece	quick
lay	man	mud(dy)	old	pile	quiet
lazy	many	music	on	pillow	quite
	map				

62

race	sandwich	silver	stain	table	time
radio	sand(y)	since	stairs (also	tail	tin
rain(y)	save	sing(er)	-stairs, e.g.	take	tired
rat	say	sir	in upstairs)	talk	to
rather	school	sister	stale	tall	today
reach	scissors	sit	stamp	tame	together
read	score	size	stand	tank	tomorrow
ready	sea	skirt	star	tap	tongue
real	seat	sky	start	taste	tonight
red	second (n.)	sleep(y)	station	tea	too
remember	see	slice	stay	teach(er)	tooth
repeat	seldom	slide	steal	team	top
rest	-self/-selves	slip(pery)	steep	tear (v.)	towards
restaurant	sell	slow	step	telegram	towel
rice	send	small	stick (n.)	telephone	tower
rich	sentence	smell	sticky	tell	town
ride	servant	smile	still	temple	toy
right	several	smoke	sting	tennis	train (n.)
ring (n.)	sew(ing)	smooth	stocking	tent	travel
ring (v.)	shade(shady)	snake	stomach	terrible	tree
river	shake	snow	stone	than	trip
road	shallow	so	stop	thank	trouble
roar	shape	soap	storm(y)	that/those	trousers
rock	sharp	sock	story	the	truck
roll	she	soft	stove	theatre	true
roof	shed	soldier	straight	then	try
room	sheep	some	strange	there	turn
rope	sheet	sometimes	street	they	twice
rose	shelf	son	string	thick	type (v.)
rough	shilling	song	strong	thief	typist
round	shine	soon	student	thin	
row (v.)	ship	sorry	study	thing (also	ugly
rub	shirt	soup	stupid	-thing, e.g.	umbrella
rubber	shoe	sour	such	in nothing)	uncle
rug	shoot	south	suddenly	think	under
ruler	shop(keeper)	speak	sugar	thirsty	understand
run	short	spell	sum	this/these	university
	shorts	spend	summer	through	until
	shout	spill	sun(ny)	throw	up
sad	show	spoil	surprised	ticket	useful
safe	shut	spoon(ful)	sweep	tidy	useless
sail	shy	sport	sweet	tie	usually
salt	sick	spring (n.)	swim(mer)	tiger	
same	side	square	sword	till	valley

van	*wall*	*weather*	*which*	*wing*	*wrong*
vegetable	*want*	*week*	*while*	*winter*	
very	*warm*	*weigh*	*white*	*wipe*	*yard*
village	*wash*	*well (a.)*	*who*	*wire*	*year*
visit(or)	*watch (n.)*	*west*	*why*	*with(out)*	*yellow*
volley-ball	*watch (v.)*	*wet*	*wide*	*woman*	*yes*
voyage	*water*	*what*	*wife*	*wood*	*yesterday*
	wave	*wheel*	*wild*	*wool*	*yet*
	way	*when(ever)*	*will (v.)*	*word*	*you*
wait	*we*	*where* (also	*win*	*work*	*young*
wake	*weak*	-*where*, e.g.	*window*	*world*	
walk(ing stick)	*wear*	in *nowhere*)	*wind(y)*	*write*	*zoo*